Let's Go to the Store!

grocery store

PRICES YOU CAN TRUST.
1 99

bananas
bread
sandwich
cake

store
Casual
Casual
Casual
Jeans
Jacken
$19,99
$14,99
$24,99
$24,99
$12,99
big labels small prices
60%

$19.99

shoes
socks
shorts
shoes

book store

BARGAIN BOOKS
new books added daily
We supply the frame...
You insert the diploma.

crayons
Max
Goes Shopping
by Adria F. Klein
illustrated by
Mernie Gallagher-Cole
NATIONAL GEOGRAPHIC
Windows on Literacy™
Shopping with Dad
Lesley Pether
books